T0156984

32 Sales Objections Easily Countered

32 Sales Objections Easily Countered

A Quick and Easy Guide to Countering the Most Common Sales Objections, Stalls, and Pushbacks with Words That Work

Stepp Stevens Sydnor

iUniverse

**32 SALES OBJECTIONS EASILY COUNTERED
A QUICK AND EASY GUIDE TO COUNTERING THE
MOST COMMON SALES OBJECTIONS, STALLS,
AND PUSHBACKS WITH WORDS THAT WORK**

iUniverse books may be ordered through booksellers or by contacting:

*iUniverse
1663 Liberty Drive
Bloomington, IN 47403
www.iuniverse.com
1-800-Authors (1-800-288-4677)*

*Because of the dynamic nature of the Internet, any web addresses or
links contained in this book may have changed since publication and
may no longer be valid. The views expressed in this work are solely those
of the author and do not necessarily reflect the views of the publisher,
and the publisher hereby disclaims any responsibility for them.*

*Any people depicted in stock imagery provided by Thinkstock are
models, and such images are being used for illustrative purposes only.
Certain stock imagery © Thinkstock.*

*ISBN: 978-1-4917-7451-9 (sc)
ISBN: 978-1-4917-7450-2 (e)*

Library of Congress Control Number: 2015913629

Print information available on the last page.

iUniverse rev. date: 10/07/2015

Contents

PRAISE FOR STEPP STEVENS SYDNOR

"Stepp's hard-earned expertise is so simple yet so profound. Practice the art of countering objections, and a year from today everything 'sales' will change in your organization!"
—Pamela Walters, executive vice president, the Devine Group, Inc.

"Stepp provides truly insightful feedback that only someone with an extremely high conceptual understanding of the sales process can provide. His coaching during the implementation of our new sales process has been invaluable not only to my sales team but to me as the manager."
—Elliott Gray, sales manager, Comcast Business

"It has been my pleasure to work with Stepp for over five years. He is indeed the true professional in every aspect of his work."
—Ron Howell, Action Business Consulting

"Stepp Sydnor has the secret sauce needed to maximize meaningful sales success. He can help unlock hidden opportunities and drive meaningful results."
—Sean Lofton, sales director, SMB Outside Sales, Comcast Business

"Stepp's methods work. Those who use them excel."
—Dave Pickens, CEO/owner, Cynergy Technology

"Stepp's unique and distinctive approach in handling objections significantly simplifies the sales process ... Well worth the time spent to listen to his techniques!"
—Claudia Hernandez, sales manager, Comcast Advanced Services

"Stepp, you brought us into the twenty-first century with an extremely effective sales process. Thank you, my friend!"
—Matt Nellenback, president, Leon's Signs Inc.

"I never spend time with Stepp Sydnor that I don't leave thinking at a higher level. I know this book will do the same for all who want to learn about sales and how to succeed in this vital area of life."
—Kim Beckham, author of *Hidden Dangers: Combating Threats to Healthy Relationships*, speaker, and performance coach

"Having worked with Stepp at two companies now, I can tell that his techniques are proven and time tested!"
—Steve Walsh, regional vice president, Comcast

"Stepp's ability to process large amounts of information and articulate it in a simple and understandable format is benchmark!"
—Hildred White, business consultant

"Stepp is a great storyteller ... If you haven't heard Stepp tell one of his stories, then you are missing out. Stepp's stories are filled with life lessons and business savvy, which I frequently use when coaching my sales teams. Gets results and many times even a laugh out loud."
—Connie White, sales consultant and coach

"Stepp brings a straightforward approach to the sales process. Through proven tools and tactics, Stepp has created a repeatable blueprint to deliver daily results."
—Elton Hart, national field sales senior director, Comcast

"Thanks to Stepp's 2MeetingClose Seminars, by adding a success story, my sales have increased 25 percent in one month's time."
—Doug Million, 1st Choice Personnel

"I just finished your program! It was a marvelous program that taught me a tremendous amount. I've begun implementing as many of your principles as I can and seeing positive results."
—Eric R. Armstrong, Texas Realtor

"Stepp's programs consistently deliver results. In session after session I've seen his audiences come alive with the understanding of how they can apply the principles of sales, communication, and relationship building in order to excel in the work they do each day. He gives you the tools to naturally master and grow confident in the sales process, *and* he is a delight to work with!"
—Jordan Mercedes, RePurpose Work

"Stepp in a word? *Amazing!* He is a master at teaching communication and negotiation skills that have had a tremendous impact on my ability to retain customers."
—Jim Hayden, account manager, Cox Business Services, Rancho Santa Margarita, California

"In following Stepp's approach, we effectively addressed our workplace communication problems … improved revenues from ten million to forty million. We indeed had a turnaround, thanks to his concise and doable tips for improved interaction."
—Gulam Harji, plant manager, Hood Packaging

"When it comes to using creative analogies to present new ideas, Stepp is exceptional! From 'a little bit of pressure over an extended period to time' creates desired change to C (compensation) x F (frequency) = Revenue, Stepp never leaves the participant without a nugget to reinforce the learning."
—Shirley Askew, president, Q Unlimited Performance Management Consulting

"Stepp's top-producer approach helped us become the number-one store out of 455 Sam's Club stores nationwide!"
—George Cunningham, Sam's Club

"By implementing Stepp's awesome sales coaching strategies and tactics, our market has increased 17 percent over the last couple of months. I am so thankful for the guidance and direction and will never go back to my old ways of coaching."
—Jonathan Ray, field sales manager, Comcast

"Thank you so much for wonderful, detailed classes. I learned a lot and have increased my real estate business! I highly recommend this information to seasoned and new agents!"
—Barbara Curry, Realtor, SFR, CFS

To my grandchildren,
Jackson and Sylvie Sydnor

SPECIAL THANKS

I would like to thank the following people, who have helped to inspire me, encourage me, and keep me motivated on this project. Thank you to my wife, Misty, for spending precious time during the evening editing this manuscript. You are wonderfully amazing. To my book-writing accountability team, Randy Stevenson and Kim Beckham, you have been so valuable in keeping me on task as well as offering up great ideas. And special thanks to Bobbie Woods. If you didn't singlehandedly manage our customers' needs, I couldn't have done much of any of this.

Part I: The Basics

Prospect and buyer objections are just part of the sales job.

During my thirty-five years in the business of selling, I experienced almost every objection imaginable. I started as an account representative for a technology distributor, selling motherboard component parts and mil-spec connectors. The company gave me absolutely no sales training and a territory that had zero customers. My target buyers were purchasing agents for the defense industry. In my first year, I made many mistakes and collected a hundred nos for every yes (or at least it seemed like it). Because of my need to support a young family, quitting wasn't an option. My saving grace, and eventual success, was due to a sales mentor I'd sought out as well as investing my own resources in books and seminars and growing from my mistakes.

I had to realize that buyers object to just about everything. And the more seasoned the buyers, the more intelligent their strategies. I was clueless when I started in sales. Objections from potential buyers felt like personal attacks on my character. I found that getting a meeting was very easy and that most buyers would agree to meet with me. However, I wasn't prepared for the buyer/seller politics and negotiation tactics used by buyers and prospects. Through bad experiences and more losses than wins, I began to understand the importance of mastering sales techniques. And one skill set I needed the most was countering buyer objections.

It's just the way the selling world works. Prospect and buyer objections are part of the job. So before we get started, let's review a few quick basics you need in order to be equipped to counter sales objections effectively.

You need to love selling. If you don't, find something else to do with your life. If you don't know what type of sales job will best fit your personality, e-mail me at stepp@2meetingclose.com, and I'll help you discover it.

You need to believe in yourself because confidence sells.

You need to believe that your product or service provides a solution that helps your buyers.

You need to be able to manage conflict in a way that doesn't cause you to cry or to lose your cool.

You need to be prepared and to be able to think fast on your feet.

You need to learn an effective sales meeting process that looks professional and keeps you on track. Check out my website www.2meetingclose.com on how to do an effective meeting.

You need to read everything you can about the art of selling.

You need to be able to stand in front of a group of potential prospects and to present well. Find a Toastmasters group in your area and join.

You need a lot of ambition and drive, which means you need a strong desire to win and to be the best you can be.

You need a seasoned sales mentor to challenge how you think and give you tons of encouragement.

Is This the Best
Price I Can Get?

As I was developing a seminar on how to counter objections, I needed an exercise to help salespeople understand the need to be prepared. I started with two thoughts:

- How well do I object to a vendor as a prospect?
- How well can I counter an objection from a prospect?

So I decided to do an exercise. Here's what I did. For the next few days, every time I purchased something from *anyone*, I planned to ask that person, "Is this the best price I can get?"

Yes, I did say *anyone*. I started at a coffee shop I like to go to. My objective was to see how the employees would respond to a price objection.

While standing in line at the coffee shop, knowing I was going to object to the price, I began having an inner struggle with myself and almost gave up the idea. I mean, who would ask this question at a coffee shop? When I got to the counter, here's what happened:

"What can I get you?" the barista asked.

"I would like a tall [that's a small in layman's terms] coffee," I said. "But before you ring it up, I have one question."

"Sure," she said, "what's the question?"

"Is this the best price I can get?"

"What? The coffee is only a dollar fifty-two," she said with a startled, confused look—not to mention the expressions of other customers, who were apparently shocked by my audacity and rudeness.

"I just want to know, is this the best price I can get?" I asked again.

Her pause seemed like an eternity as she stared at me and then looked at the other customers, who were just as interested in her response.

She said, "Um, let me get the manager."

The store manager came out from the back, walking slowly with the barista while she explained the situation to him. Turning to me, he asked, "Can I help you?"

"Yes. I was just asking the barista, before she rang up my coffee, if this is the best price I can get."

With a bewildered look that you get from someone who is having a brain freeze, he said, "Well ... uh ... here, just have it for free."

"Well, thank you," I happily replied. And I walked out with a free cup of coffee.

Afterward, I was wondering why the barista and the manager couldn't handle this simple but common objection. So I decided to try this again at the same coffee shop the next day.

Day two: different barista, same manager.

"Can I help you?" the barista asked.

"Yes," I said. "I would like a tall coffee with a little room for cream. But before you ring it up, I have one question."

"What do you need?" she asked.

"I'm wondering if this is the best price I can get."

As you can imagine, everyone in line behind me went quiet. All attention was now on me. Honestly, I'm not sure what was going through the barista's head as she was trying to process my request. After a long pause, she asked, "Are you serious? You want a better price?"

"I'm just asking," I said. "Is something wrong?"

The barista didn't even reply. She turned, left the cash register, and went through a door to the back room. After a few moments, the manager came out and said, "Are you asking us again if this is the best price you can get?"

"Yes, I sure am," I politely said. "I was just wondering if this is the best price I can get."

The manager laughed and said, "Here, man, it's free."

What I found interesting is that the barista and the manager simply didn't know how to counter a simple price objection. I had made some discoveries:

- The staff were not prepared to counter the objection, so they had to get the manager.
- The manager wasn't prepared to counter the objection, so he defaulted to giving his product away.
- The audience wasn't expecting this nutcase to hold up the line by asking for a discount.

The point here is this:

- When you are the prospect, do you negotiate well for your own purchases? And do you object to vendors' offers in order to sharpen your own countering skills?
- When you are a salesperson, do you know how to counter objections effectively and quickly?

In either situation, this book will help you effectively counter sales objections and grow your personal income.

EFFECTIVE COUNTERS WILL GROW YOUR SALES INCOME

If you are in a business-to-business sales role, including retention sales, inside or outside, account management, consultative, transactional commodity, or value selling, this book will help you increase your sales income. Sales professionals make their living convincing buyers to convince themselves they need a product or service. The sky is the limit on income potential (not to mention the freedom we experience being out and about and not sitting behind a desk all day). However, not every month is a great month for sales and commissions. This means that with just about every deal, you will encounter people who just say no or maybe. You need to answer customer objections effectively in order to turn nos and maybes into more yeses to ensure your future income.

This book will help you overcome the most common sales objections I've seen. Sales objections are part of your selling success. And since selling success is your goal, choose to be exceptional at answering buyer objections. Answering objections is something you learn to love because your financial income depends on your ability to navigate quickly through them. Developing the ability to respond quickly to objections will help you stabilize and grow your income.

There are millions of salespeople on the streets right now trying to sell their goods and services. There are millions of phone calls being placed right now in hopes of getting an appointment or moving a deal forward toward a decision. Keep this in mind while making your own sales calls. Prospects, buyers, and gatekeepers have their own work to get done, and unless you have a compelling reason to meet with them, they will object to your request.

Every stage of the sales process is filled with objections from the prospect or current customer. When you get a prospect on the phone and ask for a meeting, you'd better anticipate objections. When you ask for an order to close a deal, you'd better anticipate objections—for example, when you're networking at an event, trying to get the decision maker to meet with you. You'd better anticipate and expect objections.

ANTICIPATE AND EXPECT OBJECTIONS, BECAUSE THEY ARE COMING

It's a soon-to-be financially broke salesperson that doesn't anticipate an objection. A linebacker on a football team anticipates the hit and therefore is ready for the impact. A jet pilot anticipates turbulence when in flight and therefore isn't surprised when the plane bounces around. In a like manner, you need to anticipate and be ready for objections. Every objection is a defensive hit. Effectively countering objections is an opportunity to change the buyer's mind-set, so be ready.

As a salesperson and now a communicator of sales strategies, I am frequently surprised by how many really good salespeople do not spend time developing their ability to negotiate a sales objection. Many think they will be ready the moment an objection happens. When a prospect says, "I have a better price from another vendor" or "Let me think about it," they answer without thinking.

Salesperson: "So let's move this deal forward."

Prospect: "I have a better price from another vendor."

Salesperson: "Oh, okay … Let me knock off another 20 percent."

Prospect: "Let me think about it."

Salesperson: "Okay, you think about it, and I will call you next week."

Prospect: "No, I will call you."

Salesperson: "Okay, call me when you're ready."

This is tragic! These ridiculous responses cost you and your company time and money, which causes you to lose deals and personal income—not to mention how much harder you will have to work.

Do you really want to work harder? I hope not. This is why I wrote this book: to help you respond to objections effectively and quickly.

How to Use This Book

I have identified thirty-two of the most difficult and typical types of objections, along with suggested counters. To get you started, consider these six important "Stepps."

Stepp One: Anticipate Objections

You need to anticipate that the prospect *will* push back and object. Make it your goal to develop a superior objection-countering mind-set. This mind-set prepares you for future sales objections. You can't know what the customer is thinking, but you can anticipate their objections and be ready to respond. Anticipating objections will cause your mind to think and practice possible conversations *before* they happen. Much as a musician practices before performing for an audience or a football team practices before a game, when you anticipate objections, you prepare yourself to be able to counter them.

Stepp Two: Learn to Minimize and Redirect Objections

If you anticipate sales objections, you will be able to quickly and efficiently minimize them. Minimizing is the art of making prospects' objections appear insignificant to them and also making the objections not the *only* issue. You will be more confident and will not freeze when customers push back at you. Be ready to negotiate the conversation so that you and your clients can discover why your product or service is a good fit for them.

Stepp Three: Role-Play

If you anticipate that a prospect is going to object, you should be writing down possible objections and role-playing. You can minimize and redirect those objections only through effective role-playing.

For example, when boxers anticipate punches, they are better able to minimize the impact of the hits—and, in many cases, avoid a knockout. However, imagine if they didn't spend time preparing. The dream of winning big would be just a dream. This is the same principle when dealing with sales objections. Practice through role-playing. You will be able to naturally and comfortably counter every objection like a possible hit, minimize the impact, and win the match.

Stepp Four: Choose to Improve Your Personal Skill Set

Invest in your own education. Use this book as a guide to improve your personal skills at answering customer objections. You may be working as an entrepreneur or independent agent and need to fund your own education. This book is your best resource. I suggest a steady diet of reading and practicing by using this book daily.

Try this exercise:

Imagine you are in a sales meeting, and the customer offers an objection. How will you respond?

Imagine you are the prospect, and you use that objection. Ask yourself why you would use this specific objection.

Next, write your answer down; then read the suggested counter in the following chapters. There can be multiple ways to counter an objection, so I will teach you different ways. The more you practice, the more effective you will be in the selling field.

Stepp Five: Get a Workout Buddy

Another successful method is to find someone who also wants to improve his or her skills and can meet frequently with you for your own personal objection workshop. Practice until you can respond quickly and effectively.

Stepp Six: Inspire Sales Team Discussions

Sales managers can use this book for coaching and development in sales meetings. Take one or two sales objections, and offer them up for discussion in your sales meetings.

Remember—the more you practice, the better able you are to handle sales objections effectively.

OBJECTIONS SHOULDN'T BE ARM-WRESTLING MATCHES

Answering sales objections doesn't mean arm wrestling a prospect until you win. If people are interested in what you're selling, in most cases they're going to offer some kind of objection. When the customer raises an objection, don't start an arm-wrestling match.

I was in a mall during the holiday season, browsing around while my daughter and son were doing what teenagers do: shopping with the money Dad gave them. I was standing in front of a clothing store, looking at seasonal fashions for men, when I heard a woman trying to get the attention of a shopper.

"Hey, mister … hey … you."

I turned slightly to my right and looked over my shoulder, and I realized I was the person she was talking to.

"Are you talking to me?" I asked.

"Yes," the salesperson said, smiling. "Do you need a new cell phone?"

This is when I realized I was being solicited by a cell phone salesperson in a kiosk in the middle of the aisle. *Nice person,* I thought. *Aggressive, friendly, pleasant voice, and she got my attention.* I imagine she could have been thinking she was a great salesperson because she possessed certain necessary sales traits. What she may not have realized was how much commission she lost that day because she didn't know how to effectively counter my objection. Let me share with you a few things she didn't know about my cell phone situation.

I've had the same flip cell phone for almost five years. Yes, I know—after one year it's a dinosaur; my kids remind me every time they see me use it. (I happen to like dinosaurs.) My cell contract is up for renewal, so there's nothing keeping me from upgrading. I'm thinking often of getting an upgrade from my current phone to a new phone. My problem is that I know what every button on my phone does. Having to stop and learn something new is frustrating for me. I'm a creature of habit, so I'm comfortable with my little phone. It's like a family member to me. It's old, but I'm familiar with it.

I don't have e-mail capabilities on my phone, so an upgrade is something I'm interested in. I've found that texting is how my kids prefer to communicate, so a better keyboard would be helpful. And I'm very frustrated with the cell phone service of the national carrier I use. On top of that, in the middle of a conversation, the cell line often drops. When I say often, I mean every day. The bottom line is that my experience with my cell provider has not been good. So I'm somewhat frustrated.

Do you get the picture now?

I have a need to buy a new phone, and I am unhappy with my current provider. I'm a prime candidate for a new phone order. Now, back to my story.

The salesperson knows nothing about my current cell phone situation, and she works for the cell phone carrier I use. So here is how the conversation went:

Salesperson: "Hey mister … hey … you."

Me: "Are you talking to me?"

Salesperson: "Yes, do you need a new cell phone?"

Me: "Yes, I do."

Salesperson: "Great! We have lots of great deals going on."

Me (interrupting her sales pitch): "Oh yeah, I use your company already, but I do not like your service."

Salesperson: "What? Sure you like our service … We are the best."

Me: "Well, I'm not feeling like you're the best, because I don't like the service I'm getting. The line drops all the time."

Salesperson: "How old is your phone? Maybe you need to upgrade."

Me (very friendly tone): "Miss, I just said I don't care for your service."

Salesperson (very pushy and defensive): "Have you had your phone checked out? I think that's what your problem is. So let's upgrade your phone and get it fixed."

(Now we're arm wrestling.)

Me: "Sorry, but I don't think getting a new phone is the solution to *my* problem."

I turned and walked away while she was still instructing me on how my problem wasn't their problem.

Can you see how the salesperson, by her inability to counter my objection effectively, lost a current customer who had a need and was very interested in upgrading? I wonder how many potential sales she'd lost in the last sixty days. I expect her approach sent many potential clients to another provider.

- What was it the salesperson could not see?
- Why did she feel that pushing for her point of view would help her make the sale?
- Why didn't she investigate what I needed while anticipating objections?

Here is an example of what the salesperson could have done better:

Salesperson: "Oh, I'm so sorry we aren't meeting your expectations. Can you tell me what's happening?"

Me: "When I am on a call, the line drops. This seems to happen every day."

Salesperson: "I know how frustrating that can be because that happened to me. Have you called the help desk?"

Me: "No, I'm just dealing with it until I find a new vendor."

Salesperson: "We acknowledge there has been a problem with our lines dropping calls. So I apologize for the lack of call quality. We have added more towers and soon will resolve the problem. If I can have your number, I will look into the situation and call you back with a solution and more information. Until then, are you having any phone issues other than the line dropping?"

Notice how the salesperson didn't ignore my current problem with her company but acknowledged my dissatisfaction with empathy before moving to upgrade my phone. This is the proper way to deal with an objection from a buyer.

Take care of the current frustration. Get the buyer to talk about his or her problem, and try to relate to it before changing the subject. When you do this, the buyer will be more likely to talk about other opportunities.

Make Buying Safe

Make it *safe* for prospects to talk about their concerns, and they will be open to hearing your solutions. Make it *unsafe* for the potential client, and she or he will not trust your motive. Trust and respect make the client feel safe. Make it safe for customers to tell you their concerns, and they will be open to your solutions.

Customers who do not trust your true motive will either sugarcoat their response or just pretend they're interested. They may also get aggressive and fully enter an arm-wrestling match—or shut down and simply walk away. The salesperson's problem in the example I shared is that she didn't know how to answer a customer objection from the *customer's point of view*. Prospects with objections are a perfect indicator they want to talk.

Getting an objection from a potential customer is not a bad thing. You want to identify key objections as early as possible. Not all prospects will open their purse and hand you their money without raising some concerns. However, when a prospect or client offers up an objection …

See the problem from their perspective first. Don't assume you see it from their side and finish their sentence. Don't try to prove them wrong or make them feel like their opinion isn't important.

As the salesperson, expect some pushback and be ready to give an answer quickly, confidently, and politely.

Salespeople who feel they need to arm wrestle prospects simply are not selling. They are pushing potential clients away. Stop and see the world from the prospect's viewpoint, and you will create an atmosphere of trust and respect.

Avoid Quota Obsession Disorder

Most salespeople have a sales quota they need to reach—or some kind of measurement that lets the organization know how effective they are at selling. The problem is that salespeople can become so focused on their quota that they are blind to what actually makes up the quota. This has a bad side effect.

Being obsessed with a quota takes your interest off what the client needs. A prospect can sense when a salesperson's only interest is in getting a commission. Since people act out what they think, such salespeople approach prospects just as a hungry lion approaches a lamb with a broken leg. Making the kill is all they think about.

So what is the key component to selling and answering objections? Building trust and credibility. Where trust is the rudder on a ship, credibility is the sail. These two are important to navigating through client objections. Lose these, and you have no chance of a deal.

Become a Skillful Negotiator

Answering objections is closely related to being a skillful negotiator. The best way to respond to an objection is to interpret it as a question asking for more information. However, if you react defensively to a prospect's objection, you could be leaving a lot of money lying on the table.

Knowing what to say next when an objection is offered, knowing how to negotiate the conversation, and discovering key customer power points prepares you to answer objections quickly, comfortably, easily, and effectively.

The first skill you need to develop in order to minimize objections is to *learn to listen.* Listening is an art form. It's like seeing a picture being painted in front of your eyes, so get your paintbrush ready.

Can you tell when someone is not listening to you? Sure you can. There's an awkward sense when you're having a conversation in which the other party isn't tuned in to what you're saying. What signals your attention that he or she isn't listening? Body language and tone.

A lot has been said about communication—and even more about the art of listening. As a reminder, here are a few key "painter's tools" you'll want to have with you.

- Remember the eighty-twenty rule: either on the phone or in a meeting, the prospect should be talking 80 percent of the time. You should be talking 20 percent of the time. Some think that pushing for a prospect's opinion is persuading, so they talk too much themselves; once they hear an objection, they jump into a presentation. Avoid this.
- Avoid poor listening. Beware of concentrating on what you have to say rather than on what the other person is saying.
- Avoid emotional filters. They distort what is really being said. When you get emotional, you aren't logical. When you aren't logical, you tend to draw quick conclusions.

Attentive listening involves the following:

- Be motivated to listen. Lean forward, and tune everything out except what clients say. Listen to what they *mean* more than to the actual words used.
- When you speak, it's better to ask questions concerning their objections. For example, when the salesperson heard I was frustrated with her company's service, she could have said, "Oh, I am so sorry we aren't meeting your expectation. Please tell me what has been happening."
- Do not interrupt a prospect midsentence.
- Fight distractions.

- Do not trust your memory; write down key things the prospect says.
- Maintain eye contact. Looking away communicates a lack of interest.
- React to the message, not to the person you're speaking with. When prospects say, "I have a better price from another competitor" or "I don't like your service," stay calm and really listen to the purpose or meaning behind what they are saying. If you react emotionally, the buyer takes control of the sale.
- Clarify what you heard the prospect say.
- Verify whether what you think is fact or fiction.
- Reflecting empathy about the prospect's concerns and issues is the first act of business. If you do this first, the prospect will open up to you and your solution.

WHY DO CUSTOMERS STALL?

Understanding the buyer's perspective will help you discover why customers stall and object in the first place. Buyers or prospects have their own perspectives on what their needs and wants are. Knowing how to manage their perspectives puts you in a strong position to answer their objections.

Why does a prospect stall? Here are some of the hidden reasons:

- The prospect wants a high-quality product at a fair and reasonable price.
- The prospect feels competent and has good taste. You want to respect this and act accordingly.
- The prospect would like to avoid risk and trouble.
- The prospect wants to look good for the organization.
- The prospect wants relief from unnecessary work.
- The prospect has a problem and needs a solution.
- The prospect doesn't want to change the status quo.

The salesperson, on the other hand, has a different perspective. You want to make a commission. All salespeople want this, but being good at answering objections means we need to approach prospects from their perspective.

A Simple Statement That Diffuses Objections

A very good friend of mine shared with me how he quickly diffuses objections. He simply answers almost every objection with this statement: *"That's perfect! That's why I'm here!"*

Here are a few examples:

Prospect: "I already have this service!"

Salesperson: "That's perfect because that's why I'm here."

Prospect: "I'm already under contract."

Salesperson: "That's perfect. That's why I'm here!"

Prospect: "We have already had a salesperson from your company call on us."

Salesperson: "That's perfect because that's why I'm here."

When I first heard this statement, I just laughed. Could it be that easy? For a few weeks after hearing about it, I started using it as a primer for answering objections.

Honestly, it worked. In fact, it worked so well I now encourage you to use this simple statement as a starter sentence to counter every objection.

You don't think it will work?

"That's perfect … and that's why I'm here!"

PART II: THE THIRTY-TWO OBJECTIONS

On the following pages, you'll find thirty-two sales objections and how to easily counter them. I have left enough room for you to write your counter to the objection. Then turn the page, look at the "Do Say" section, and compare your counter to the ones I have listed.

The "Don't Say" sections list some very honest counters I've heard from salespeople in the field. You may have heard some as well. Some are very funny!

If you're like me and get bored easily, you don't want to read a lot of narrative. So I made this section quick and to the point.

NOTES

Objection #1

"I want to think it over."

How would you counter this objection?

Do Say

- I understand. You want to make the best decision. What do you feel you need to think about?
- I can see that. Tell me—is it money that concerns you?
- What questions have I not answered for you?
- What part of my proposal would you like to think over?
- Can you be honest with me? You said this won't meet your needs. Am I missing something?

Don't Say

- Listen—really smart people can tell this is a good deal. And you did say you thought this solution would meet your needs. Didn't you say that? Don't lie to me now! I have met with six people today, and they all said the same thing as you. So unless you are just a big fat liar, I suggest you level with me.
- Mr. Customer, it's the end of the month. If I don't meet my quota by five today, my boss is going to be really mad, and I just may lose my job. I have nine kids all under the age of seven. Do you want me to lose my job? Let's not think it over any more. Let's say yes!

Stepp's Tip: "I want to think it over."

You need to be ready to answer this objection quickly; don't blink or hesitate. Within seconds, you must fire back a reasonable-sounding reply. The prospect is giving you honest feedback, and the message you can interpret is "I am not sold on this idea, product, or service yet." Objections are good. So see them as an opportunity to ask more questions. Try restating what the prospect just said, and then use one of the great responses provided. Practice your answer, and get comfortable with the prospect pushing back on you.

NOTES

Objection #2

"Your product is more expensive than your competitor's."

How would you counter this objection?

Do Say

- I agree we are not the low-price leader. Are you looking for a company that can offer you only the lowest price possible, or are service and quality a concern?
- Many of my clients said the same thing until we took a closer look at what features and benefits they were getting compared to what I'm offering. Can we go through the benefits of each and discover what features are best for your business?

Don't Say

- Well, duh. Of course we are. Don't you want to get the best bang for your buck? I mean, who am I competing with anyway? … Oh, them. Well, they really suck, and rumors have it they are heading into big financial problems.
- I don't like to spread rumors, but I heard that the vendor you're using is under a government investigation. Don't you think switching now is a good idea? I do! Here's a pen. Just sign right here.

Stepp's Tip: "Your product is more expensive than your competitor's."

Imagine you are the prospect and you asked a salesperson this question. Why would you ask it? Place yourself in his or her shoes and think about what's going on. People buy products all the time that cost more money than others. I know I do. So the prospect is saying, "Hey, I don't see the cost value, and my need for the product isn't motivating me enough to buy from you." Find out first from your prospects how the product will help them do something better or faster. Then use what they said when they ask this classic objection.

People buy from people they like. So use exceptional relationship skills to tip the decision scale your way. Tell the prospect, "Yes, you're right. We do charge more money, and here is why ..." Approach the client like a consultant problem solver. You'll find it easier to fire back a reply if you and the prospect are both interviewing each other to see if there is a good reason to do business together.

NOTES

Objection #3

"We aren't interested."

How would you counter this objection?

Do Say

- I can understand you not being interested on the basis of a phone call. However, we've helped many companies like yours reduce costs and improve their market size. That's the reason for getting together. I would like to introduce myself and learn more about you. I promise not to take much of your time. Can we meet for a few minutes? How is Tuesday at ten o'clock or Thursday at nine o'clock?

- Mr. Owner, I specialize in helping people in your position gain more market share using our product and service. I was just wondering if you would be interested in getting together for a few minutes to learn more about you and your business and to see if it makes sense to do business together.

Don't Say

- You can be happy the day you sign with our competitor because of the price, or you can be happy today with the quality of our product (or service) when you sign with us. It's your choice. But don't blame me when things don't work out.

- Sure, you're not interested. I mean, you don't know me. You think I'm just a stupid salesperson. But you are interested in saving money, right? Hello? Are you there?

Stepp's Tip: "We aren't interested."

If you don't create interest with prospects, why would they want to waste their time meeting with you? Creating interest in meeting with you can be frustrating when you're focused on what you want and not what the prospect wants. I'm sure you've had salespeople try to educate you on why you need to meet with them, how great their product is, and how many clients are happy with their services; however, prospects don't really care about you, your product, or your company. They care about what you, your product, or your company can do for them. The rule for answering this objection is *not* to get the objection in the first place. Think about this:

You are a small-business owner of a company that makes candles. As the owner, it's all about gaining market share. You want to get more customers and keep them. You get a call from a salesperson, who asks you, "Mr. Owner, I am Stepp with ABC Company. We are the best in the industry, and we can help you make more candles."

The point is, owners have heard this before, and you're keeping them from doing something they feel is more important than listening to another sales pitch. They feel salespeople are annoying. However, if the salesperson said, "Mr. Owner, I specialize in helping people in your position gain more market share using our product and service. I was wondering if you would be interested in …"

Now the owner is as interested as a toddler with his eye on the ice cream truck coming down the street.

NOTES

Objection #4

"We are happy with our current vendor."

How would you counter this objection?

Do Say

- Great, may I ask you what they do that you're happy with?
- I understand that these things are important to you. Do you think having a backup vendor would be helpful in the event your current supplier doesn't come through?
- That's great. Are you aware of the changes in the industry? New features? New benefits?
- Oh, thanks for telling me that. I'm here to show you a few new options that could help save you time and maybe money, which your current vendor is missing.

Don't Say

- Hey, you would be happy with me too if you gave me a chance. Please, please, please give me a chance.
- Maybe you think you're happy, but if I could see you this week, you will understand why many clients are switching to us. We are the best in this business. Don't you want to get service from the best too?

Stepp's Tip: "We are happy with our current vendor."

If you'd like to have this client in the future, keep a tickler file and follow up at a later date. Try not to burn any bridges; keep the conversation light, and follow up often. Remember—not all clients are completely happy with their current vendors. The good news is that most vendors eventually do something to disappoint their customers. Processes break down, and busy salespeople forget to follow up. Do not—and I mean *do not*—trash the other vendor. This could backfire on you. For example, you never know if the vendor is the prospect's friend or family member. Win the business by creating and bringing value to the prospect.

NOTES

Objection #5

"We just switched companies (or services)."

How would you counter this objection?

Do Say

- How long ago was the switch? What was the main reason you selected this vendor? Can you share with me the area of responsibility they will take care of and your ROI expectation? We constantly enhance our business services, and I'd like to have the opportunity to bring you up to date on how we might be able to benefit you.
- Oh, I see. When did you switch? What was the reason for the switch? I am so sorry I wasn't able to provide a proposal for that. Are you under contract? For how long? Would you be interested in looking at one of our other services that your current vendor doesn't provide? I really would hate to lose you as a customer.

Don't Say

- Oh, I am sorry you did that. You may not know this but you made a very bad decision. That company has had a big problem with taking people's deposits and not delivering the product. I am sure you will be calling me back.

Stepp's Tip: "We just switched companies (or services)."

This is a perfect time to find out why they switched. What happened that caused the prospect to switch vendors? Use this information to remind future prospects that they will avoid these issues when buying from you. Also, remember—if prospects are the type you'd like to do business with in the future, be sure to follow up with them every sixty to ninety days.

Objection #6

"Everyone is offering the same rate."

How would you counter this objection?

Do Say

- This is a very competitive industry, and therefore it may seem that way. I would like to explain the differences between my company and my competitor's company and see if we can find a fit that works best for your needs. Does that seem agreeable to you?
- Thank you. I am curious … when selecting a vendor, what else besides price is most important? Based on what you said, if I can satisfy those needs, can we meet to review how using us is possibly the best option?
- Thank you for letting me know. Not everyone can offer the same level of reliability, service, and support, so vendors can catch you off guard with price first. I'm curious how much you really know about their product quality and service?

Don't Say

- Everywhere I go, I think my competitors are following me around talking to my clients and offering them my prices. Well, you like me better, right? I mean, we've had a lot of lunches and ball games together. Honestly, you're my friend, right?

Stepp's Tip: "Everyone is offering the same rate."

I love this "same rate" sales objection. The prospect is basically asking me to give a reason to go with my company.

If the rate is the same, are the service, product, company, delivery, and technology the same? This is the perfect time to tell the prospect why your company is the best choice.

Another tip: start creating value before jumping to another discount. If you plan to discount the price, make sure you get a commitment from the prospect. Ask the prospect, "If I can get you a better value/price, will you do business with me?" If you don't get a commitment from the prospect before you make an adjustment, you may be cheating yourself out of a sale or a healthy profit margin. Why? Because the prospect will get you to make concessions and then call your competition and ask them the same thing. Be smart! Do not fall for this trap.

NOTES

Objection #7

"We're moving."

How would you counter this objection?

Do Say

- Really? That's wonderful! This is a good opportunity for you to make preparations to meet your product (or service) needs before you move. Once we review your needs, I can begin the process on my end to ensure that we meet your time requirements. The timing couldn't be better. Wouldn't you agree?

Don't Say

- Where are you moving to? Texas? Who would want to move there? That's just my opinion. Hmmm, I guess we won't be doing any more business, then. I don't service Texas.

Stepp's Tip: "We're moving."

When the prospect says, "We are moving," you want to sound excited about the move and ask where. When is the move date? What is the reason for the move? Are they growing? Are they consolidating locations? You may find they are in the perfect position to need your products or services. Also pay attention to who may be moving into their space. This also could turn into a potential sale. Be helpful as well. You may not be able to service them, but you may know someone you could refer them to.

How will you know if they are bluffing? If they're truly moving, they will answer your questions. If it's a smoke screen, they will skirt, dodge, and avoid the issue. At least then you'll know they're bluffing, and you can move on to better opportunities.

Objection #8

"I'm too busy."

How would you counter this objection?

Do Say

- I can respect that this isn't a convenient time. I honestly feel that if given fifteen minutes of your time, I can show you there is good synergy between our companies. My main goal is to show you how we can improve revenues and customer acquisition. I will be in your area next Thursday and Friday. Will either of those days work for you?
- Thank you. In light of your schedule, I understand how busy you are. Is there a better time? I've spent a lot of time reviewing your account, so we can review it quickly and make appropriate changes based on your business requirements. Can I meet with you later today or tomorrow morning?

Don't Say

- Are you too busy to save your company money? Sounds lazy to me. I'm sure you would jump at the opportunity to save money on your personal budget, so why not your business' as well? What is two minutes of listening if it saves you twenty dollars a week? That's $960 a year. Besides, when you show the boss how much money you saved the company, there is more money available for your raise.
- Get over yourself. Everyone is busy! How am I supposed to help you if you tell me you're too busy? Slow down, take time to smell the roses, and meet

with me so I can save you money. You do want to save money, don't you?

Stepp's Tip: "I'm too busy."

Don't be too pushy here. Believe them when they say, "I'm too busy." For prospects you want to do business with in the future, do the following:

- Be kind.
- Be sensitive.
- Ask if tomorrow would be better.
- Tell them you understand, and give them a good reason to see you at another time.
- Be consistent.
- Be diligent.
- Be kind … Did I say that already? Always be kind and polite.

Gentle persistence always pays off.

NOTES

Objection #9

"Your product is too complex."

How would you counter this objection?

Do Say

- Many of my best clients thought that too. I can see that I may have confused you, or you may have some information that isn't correct. Can I take a few minutes to clarify how the product will support your business needs?
- What are you comparing our product to that makes you feel that way?

Don't Say

- Plainly and simply, you won't know if something is too complex if you don't take the time to learn about it.
- I know – I think so too! I have to talk to one of our engineers to understand what the darn thing does, so I know how you feel. But the truth is that this product is just what the doctor ordered. Besides, if you buy this from me and I make quota this month, I'll be eligible for the President's Club!

Stepp's Tip: "Your product is too complex."

Listen closely to what prospects are telling you. Saying something is too complex is another way of telling you, "I don't see how your product fits into my business" or "I just don't understand all this technology language. I'm bored now, so please leave." Or they simply haven't had someone explain the product to them in a way they can understand.

Be sure you're speaking the right language to the right person. For instance, CEO-level people do not speak technology. They speak a language that deals with market share and market size. Tell them how your product or service can improve their market shares or sizes, and you have potential customers who will give you ten more minutes of their time.

Vice presidents and directors speak another language. They speak the language of improving business processes, coming in under budget, and increasing efficiency.

Managers and users speak the language of features and benefits. Since these people are closer to the actual performance line, they are the ones using the products' features and benefits.

If you speak the wrong language to any one of these people, they will be confused or bored out of their minds, which is a bad thing for you. In turn they may send a smoke signal to you: "Your product is too complex."

NOTES

Objection #10

"Call me on Monday to set up an appointment."

How would you counter this objection?

Do Say

- I have some time on Tuesday afternoon to meet with you. What time is best for you?
- How about we set up a tentative time for Tuesday, and I'll call to confirm on Monday?
- There's a promotion that ends soon, and I would like you to get the full savings and extra benefits before it expires. How about we meet either Tuesday or Wednesday of next week?
- Great! I'll call you on Monday. Let me get your e-mail address so I can send you confirmation for the appointment we set. I can see that you're busy and will call next Monday.
- I would be happy to call you back or to set up an appointment at a later time, but as a fellow business owner, I understand that calendars fill up quickly. Why don't we set up a tentative appointment now? Would Tuesday two weeks from now or Thursday two weeks from now be better for you? Nine in the morning or three in the afternoon?

Don't Say

- Okay, well, I'm busy as well, but I'm not too busy to talk to you. So why don't we just schedule it now for next Monday and be done with it, since we're both busy people? I'm available at two. Can you make that time?

Stepp's Tip: "Call me on Monday to set up an appointment."

I like this objection because the prospect has opened the door to a possible meeting. When the prospect says, "Call me Monday," make a note on your calendar and call again on Monday. When you speak to customers, remind them of the request that you call on Monday to schedule an appointment. This almost always ensures an appointment. Always be direct and up front about why you are calling. Avoid trying to sound like a long-lost friend. Prospects can tell when you're using a sales technique to get the appointment. Just be honest, direct, to the point, persistent, and polite. Do this, and you will eventually have more appointments than you know what to do with.

NOTES

Objection #11

"It's not a priority to us."

How would you counter this objection?

Do Say

- Thank you for telling me that. Are you saying it's a priority later but just not right now?
- I understand it isn't a priority now. But I'm curious whether you can fit me in sometime next week to see if I can determine if there's a possible synergy between us. If I'm not able to, I'll be the first to tell you and be on my way. Just twenty minutes is all it will take.
- I understand that my product or service is not a priority for your business. However, if I could show you a solution to streamline the day-to-day operations of your business into a more efficient and cost-effective design, would that be a priority?

Don't Say

- Maybe you wouldn't be working so late if saving time were a priority.
- I have called you once a day for six weeks. Didn't your mama tell you it's rude not to return a phone call? Come on, give me a break!

Stepp's Tip: "It's not a priority to us."

When prospects throw this objection at you, stop and put yourself in their shoes. "It's not a priority" is another way of saying, "Your request isn't at the top of my list, *but* it is on the list somewhere." Your job is to help the client move this nonpriority to a higher level. These counters from the field work well, so use them. Initiate questions quickly that get to the heart of the issue. When asking questions, remember to ask one and then wait for a response.

By the way, do you feel uncomfortable asking questions like "Are you telling me that employee loyalty to your organization is not a priority and that you don't have your employees' best interests in mind?" If this kind of question is difficult for you, consider getting out of the selling business. You may be more successful as an order taker. Why? Because selling is about, well, selling! And initiating tough questions helps prospects follow you to a solution or helps you quickly qualify them as a low probability. To be successful at answering prospect objections you need to be able to ask hard questions.

NOTES

Objection #12

"Just send me literature."

How would you counter this objection?

Do Say

- If you would like me to send literature to you, does that mean you are somewhat interested? Who else would need to see a brochure?
- Sure, I will get some information out to you right away. Do you have an idea which product you would like to review? And when I send the literature, would you be interested in meeting with me to review it?
- I could send you general information; however, we customize our services to meet your needs in order to help you get the best results. If you have a few minutes, I could show you a few things on our website. Are you interested?
- I can send you literature, but it's usually best if I can meet with you as well. Is this something we can do?
- I would be happy to do that; however, may I first ask you a few questions so that the information I send will be pertinent to your needs?

Don't Say

- Oh sure, you bet. You want me to go ahead and put it in the trash can for you too?

Stepp's Tip: "Just send me literature."

Literature is expensive to print and mail, so don't send anything in the mail until you're sure there is a real interest. In many cases, the literature you send will be dumped in the trash. If you do mail literature to prospects, be sure to follow up in a week or two. I like to follow up with, "What did you like best about the literature I sent you?" If they read it, they will have a good answer. If they didn't read it, they will feel embarrassed. Try to get a commitment from prospects to review the information within a few days. Even better, go over the literature on the phone or schedule an appointment.

Remember—if you can't get them back on the phone after you sent the literature, they most likely weren't interested in the first place. You just wasted the cost of the literature, envelope, postage, and your own time.

NOTES

Objection #13

"Our corporate headquarters makes all the decisions."

How would you answer this objection?

Do Say

- Great, thank you. Can you tell me who handles that on the local level?
- Although your company office makes the final decision, if you were to see something that could benefit your company, would you be able to make a recommendation?
- Could you give me the contact information for your corporate headquarters so I may present a proposal to them?

Don't Say

- Hey, man, I'm so sorry! I guess it's their loss.
- I guess you don't have any power at all. How does it feel to be low man on the totem pole?

Stepp's Tip: "Our corporate headquarters makes all the decisions."

Qualify early in cases where you may be dealing with a local office and decisions for your service or product are made elsewhere. The best strategy is to find someone who can champion your cause to the right people. That could be a gatekeeper or an end user that prefers your service or information they could provide. Get information that will help you get to the right person.

Once you find the right person, start a prospecting strategy that will get you noticed. Be careful that you aren't wasting time and money on an opportunity that will go nowhere. Qualify the prospect to be sure this is a good business fit for you too. Not all opportunities are *your* opportunities.

NOTES

Objection #14

"I need guaranteed results."

How would you counter this objection?

Do Say

- Perfect, that's why I'm here. I would expect the same. My company offers a full money-back guarantee if we don't meet your expectations.
- I completely agree. There is no risk on your part. None whatsoever. Is this your only reason not to move forward?
- No problem! All successful clients feel the same way. I can understand your need for proven results. Has there been a problem with unmet expectations in the past?
- I can guarantee the results as long as you agree to do the things we discuss.

Don't Say

- If you need a guarantee, buy an insurance policy! I mean, I don't have control of everything.

Stepp's Tip: "I need guaranteed results."

Prospects use this objection for several reasons:

- They don't want to look bad to their boss.
- They've been burned in the past.
- They want an escape clause just in case.
- They want the security of knowing you believe in your own product.

Prospects that use this objection need you to be a partner, so be sure to use words like *we* and *us*. This will feel more collaborative. Make your prospects feel safe by explaining how the warranty or guarantee will benefit them. Buyers don't want to feel trapped if your product or service doesn't meet their expectations. So offering "money back" or "cancellation in thirty days" will help you close deals faster.

NOTES

"I tried your product before, and it didn't work."

How would you counter this objection?

Do Say

- I'm sorry. What happened? How did you use it? What was the result? What could have been done better?
- I know how you feel. Let me ask you, have you ever had a meal at a restaurant that didn't meet your expectations? Does that mean you would never eat at the restaurant again? Maybe your last experience with this product was like that. Could we start over?
- I'm very sorry and understand your frustration. We have several clients in your industry that use this product (or service) without any issues. Do you think it would be okay to revisit it and see how we can improve things?

Don't Say

- When did you use my product? Everyone loves it! Are you sure you were using it correctly? A lot of people your age just need more training.

Stepp's Tip: "I tried your product before, and it didn't work."

This is a common objection when someone has used your product before and didn't have a very good experience. I bought a car once that was a complete lemon; however, the manufacturer has made improvements over the years, and today the same company is a leading car producer. The point is, when prospects have had a bad experience, get them to share with you what went wrong. Don't argue with them about their experience, because you will be fighting a losing battle. Empathize with your prospects and focus on what happened. Show you care by listening to what made their experiences less than perfect.

NOTES

Objection #16

"How can you service multiple accounts? I don't want to get lost."

How would you counter this objection?

Do Say

- Your company is very important to us, and that's why we have an assigned team of specialists to manage your specific needs. There are approximately four members assigned to your account, so you can see the ratio is quite good. And these resources are available to us both, so that I can manage your accounts.

Don't Say

- Oh, don't you worry about it. You can trust me!

Stepp's Tip: "How can you service multiple accounts? I don't want to get lost."

Your prospects are looking for security, and security is what you need to give them. Many customers want "service after the sale," meaning they bought a product or service trusting they were going to get an acceptable level of service after the purchase. Poor service experiences lead a prospect to question how you can service so many accounts. It's not an objection that comes up often. However, if this question is asked and you are indifferent about it, you could possibly tip the scales away from you and toward your competition.

Objection #17

The decision maker won't return your calls.

How would you counter this objection?

Do Say

- (To the gatekeeper) Hi, my name is Stepp Sydnor. Can you help me? I am trying to get a meeting with Mr. Diehard and seem to be having a difficult time getting an appointment. Is there a better way to do this? What's your advice?
- (On voice mail) Hi, Mr. Diehard, I know how busy you are. In our last meeting, you asked me to get back with you today. When you get a free minute, please call me on my cell phone. That number is 818-888-9988. Thank you, I will try you again later.

Don't Say

- (To a gatekeeper) Hey, cutie, your boss and I have been playing phone tag. He is insistent that I get in touch with him so how about you be a good receptionist and get him on the phone for me?
- (On voicemail) You must be ignoring my phone calls. I have left several messages for you with no response. You have until close of business Friday to take advantage of the low cost deal we discussed. If I don't hear from you, it's your loss man.

Stepp's Tip: The decision maker won't take your calls.

Do you actually expect decision makers to drop everything they're doing and call you? If so, you need to get out of this business. This is why we call it "sales." You need to get creative and stay determined as well as stay polite and kind.

Too aggressive and you're toast. Too soft and you'll give up too early.

If you are prospecting and trying to get the decision maker to see you, try something different. One time I sent the general manager of a radio station an old cowboy boot filled with goodies (candy, a gift card to a coffee shop, playing cards, etc.) with a note that said, "Howdy. I've determined I have something to help you improve your sales. I have traveled a long way to see you. Can we meet? If so, I will bring the other boot."

Decision makers are busy. So be consistent and tenacious. People respect your diligence. Also, never expect that they will call you back. If you have this expectation, you will only disappoint yourself. If you keep calling once a week for seven weeks, eventually someone will reach out to you and say:

- Stop calling (usually an assistant).
- Yes, sorry I've been busy, but let's meet soon (so you will stop calling).
- Yes, let's meet. Are there any more salespeople like you? Because I need some on my team.

NOTES

Objection #18

"Why do you want copies of my bills?"

How would you counter this objection?

Do Say

- People have often told me how confusing their bills are. One of the objectives for our meeting is to help clarify what you are paying for and see if we can change anything to improve the service and possibly reduce the cost. Does that sound like something that can help you?
- This is so I can make sure we aren't missing something. I also want to identify exactly what you're getting from your current vendor.

Don't Say

- Wow, I really struck a nerve with you. Are you hiding something? Hey, I just asked to see your records so I can show you how much you may be getting ripped off. Gee, sorry I asked.

Stepp's Tip: "Why do you want copies of my bills?"

As a salesperson, in many industries, you will often want to see a customer's past billing records so you can present a sales proposal that includes or exceeds the products or services they are currently receiving. Customers can become suspicious because they don't understand your true motive. Let them know what your motive is, and most prospects will hand over the goods. If they feel you're pulling a sales trick, they'll throw up a wall of rejection.

If they object to giving you their bill(s), just assume they're concerned about you seeing what they're paying. Let your prospects know that they can mark out the pricing if that's their concern. In many situations, the buyer will find it a hassle marking out the price and will just deliver the bill(s) to you.

Objection #19

"Let me check with my partner/husband/wife."

How would you counter this objection?

Do Say

- I understand! I will note on the contract that it is subject to his (or her) approval. May I note on your account that you've okayed that? Once we get the second okay, we'll be ready to proceed.
- I'm curious if this is something *you* want to do. Is this a product or service that will help *you*? If so, can we meet with your partner now?
- If you feel that this is a good idea for your business, will your partner say yes as well?
- When do you plan to meet with your partner? Can I call you this afternoon and confirm the start date?
- What questions will he (or she) have? Let's talk about them now.
- When will it be convenient for us to get together again? I'd like him (or her) to be there as well.

Don't Say

- Really? You aren't important enough to pull the trigger?
- I hate being tied down and made to feel like I can't think for myself. Can't you just make a good decision and tell your partner how it's going to be?
- Hey, it's more fun to ask for forgiveness than permission, right?

Stepp's Tip: "Let me check with my partner/husband/ wife."

Prequalify before the meeting what the decision-making process is and confirm who will be present for the meeting. For sales where a spouse is usually involved, prequalification is especially necessary.

NOTES

Objection #20

"The economy and slow business are hurting our company."

How would you counter this objection?

Do Say

- Then I'm glad I came to see you today! I have some specific plans that will help increase business. I can show you how to move more products despite the economy.
- What are you currently doing to improve your situation? Let me show you what we're doing to help other companies like yours improve business.
- I understand. I can show you how, in many economic slowdowns, the companies that rethink how they're going to market always do better. Let me show you what we're doing to help companies like yours.
- Thanks, that's why I'm here. People are still buying, and they should be buying from you. Let's take a look at what you're currently doing and see how we can meet your customers' needs with my products.
- Do you think you're reacting to the notion that nobody is buying? People still have money to spend; let's make sure they know to come to you.

Don't Say

- Why the heck are you in business? Whining and complaining isn't going to help. Put your big-kid pants on and deal with it.

Stepp's Tip: "The economy and slow business are hurting our company."

When hard economic times hit businesses, owners are generally uncertain and stall on new ideas or services. Be sure to have success stories you can share about individuals who, despite economic downturns, have done well. For example, did you know that Microsoft and Hewlett Packard started in a depressed economy?

NOTES

Objection #21

"My budget is already spent."

How would you counter this objection?

Do Say

- If we put the budget aside for a moment, how much would the company need to get back as a return on the investment to justify the cost?
- Do you mean the budget is already spent, or do you mean it is already allocated?
- In our last conversation, you said you had control over your department's budget. Do you believe the program (or product) will bring you more business? If not, why? If so, can we move or adjust the budget?
- If you had the budget, would you do the program?

Don't Say

- It takes money to make money! Can you print a copy of your budget and let me analyze it?
- Hey, there are two kinds of people in the world: winners and losers! If you want to be a winner, you're going to have to take a risk.

Stepp's Tip: "My budget is already spent."

When buyers use this objection, it can mean one of two things:

- They really don't have the money.
- They don't want to put the money into your product or solution.

In either case, ask the buyer questions about the business. This will give you an idea where the value is. Buyers buy because your solution solves a business problem. If you don't ask questions about the business—such as "Who is your competition and how are you positioning the company to grow more market share?"—you won't know how to work yourself into their budgets.

NOTES

Objection #22

"Your rates are too high."

How would you counter this objection?

Do Say

- I understand. That's why I'm here! Can you tell me why you feel the rate is too high?
- I agree that other providers' prices are lower than mine, but our price is our price. Is there a reason you haven't already placed this order with them? Let's talk about the differences in our services.
- We service 55 percent of the market in your area. And most companies tell us our price value is lower than that of other vendors. Can you give me an idea why you feel our rates are too high?
- You're saying the price is too high, right? Then which part of my proposal do you feel you can work without?

Don't Say

- You know, it's your loss if you don't take this deal. Other vendors are less expensive because their service is horrible. I'm pretty sure I heard a rumor that your current provider is going out of business anyway.
- Why do you think people prefer quality over price? Any smart person can see that we are number one in the marketplace.

Stepp's Tip: "Your rates are too high."

In a highly competitive market, this is a common objection. The knee-jerk reaction is to discount the service. Don't do this. Instead, create value. Clients will pay for value. Another idea is to put their current business goals at risk by helping them to see what happens if they don't buy your product.

"Business is good. Why do I need this?"

How would you counter this objection?

Do Say

- Thanks for asking me that. That's why I'm here. We have a track record of improving business results a minimum of 20 percent, even when business is good. If you have a few minutes, we can discuss your current situation, and I can tell you more about what we are doing and see if it makes sense to do business together.

Don't Say

- Great! I'll let people know that so they won't be coming in here offering you anything since business is SO good.
- I hear you! Business is good for maybe you. But it could be better right?

Stepp's Tip: "Business is good. Why do I need this?"

When a prospect's business is doing well, they typically won't be interested in changing what is currently working for them. You need to get the focus off the status quo and direct the conversation in your favor with these questions:

- When business was not doing good what was the reason?
- Now that business is doing good can you share with me what you're doing different?

- How is your competition doing? And how are they insuring their future success?
- What is the benefit to the business future if there was a solution to sustain business success? Would you be open to a discussion around this solution?

NOTES

Objection #24

"I can't afford it."

How would you counter this objection?

Do Say

- Perfect, I'm glad you said that. Many of my current clients had the same concern in the beginning. Are you saying that if you could afford it, this is something you would seriously consider?
- I understand you can't afford it, and I don't want you to go over budget. Is this service or product something you would do if you had the money? Yes? Then I have some terms that will fit your budget.
- If you work with a plan we create together, we can generate revenue for your company five times what you're spending on the product. Here's a success story from one of our other clients.
- Well, the good news is that it sounds like you're interested in our product (or service); is that safe to say?

Don't Say

- Come on, you can do better than that ole standby objection. Are you a business college graduate? Sounds like you need help from a financial business consultant to get your finances in order.

Stepp's Tip: "I can't afford it."

Be sure in the first meeting or discussion that you test the client's ability to purchase. Qualify your clients by asking them if they have purchased a service like this in the past. What did they spend? What was their experience? Be sure to give them a high and low dollar number to prepare them for the investment so that it isn't a shock.

I like to say, "Have you used outside consultants in the past? Are you familiar with fees charged by training companies? Based on what you told me, an initial proposal would be $5,000 on the low end and $15,000 on the high end. Is this what you were expecting?" If they fall out of their chair and grab their chest, you know they don't have the money for your product and you are wasting your time.

NOTES

Objection #25

"You are the third rep who has called me in six months."

How would you counter this objection?

Do Say

- Well, that is why I'm calling now. I can see how frustrating this must be for you. We are just so excited about this opportunity that we've all been trying to show as many people we can about it. Can I ask you a few questions? Would you have time to meet and give me your opinion about this opportunity?
- I understand. We have a lot of marketing initiatives going on. If I were you, I would feel the same way. Establishing a relationship takes time. That's what I'm here to do with you.
- Each quarter our company identifies key companies that are positioned for growth. It looks like your company has been selected more than once. I'm sorry about the duplication. I know that's frustrating. While I'm here, can I ask you a few questions? How is your company positioned for growth in the next three to six months?

Don't Say

- Is this a problem for you? People do change jobs, you know. Just be happy our company wants to do business with you.
- You seem kind of sensitive about this. I mean, geez, give me a break.

Stepp's Tip: "You are the third rep who has called me in six months."

Imagine you have a small business and in one month four different account representatives from the same company drop by. As a salesperson, you're going to get some misplaced aggression from the prospect. Your first response is to empathize. Beware of "I'm sorry" statements. Don't apologize; empathize. Say you "understand," and tell them why you understand, such as "I know this is frustrating. I would feel the same way if I were bombarded with too many sales calls from the same company."

NOTES

Objection #26

"The home office won't let me."

How would you counter this objection?

Do Say

- Thank you for letting me know that. I have one question: Can you direct me to the person I should speak with at the home office?
- I appreciate the information. Can you advise me what I should do to get an audience with the right people at the home office?
- If you could make the decision, is this a service or product you would choose? Why or why not?

Don't Say

- There is an exception to every rule. How do we break the rules and think outside the box?
- There are leaders and there are followers. Which are you?
- Let's call them right now and let me do all the talking.

Stepp's Tip: "The home office won't let me."

This objection is either true or false. Ask this question to discover if what they are saying is a reality or just a stall: "What is the process your company goes through to make a purchase like this?"

This question will help you understand what's behind the objection.

Objection #27

"Call me next month."

How would you counter this objection?

Do Say

- I will be happy to follow up with you in a month. I have one question: Can I send you a calendar invite through my e-mail system with a date in mind?
- It seems I haven't done a very good job explaining why we should meet and why next month could be too late for you to take advantage of the specials I have to offer.

Don't Say

- You're not saying that to get me to leave, are you? Just take a minute to look at my plan.
- You're busy and so am I. Let's set up a time right now and stop dillydallying around. Time is money!

Stepp's Tip: "Call me next month."

This is a very common response. A reason they may not want to meet now is because they don't see a good enough reason to meet with you at all. Be sure to highlight the business benefits other companies are getting from your solution. The best technique is to use a verbal success story. Verbal success stories get people's attention; however, they have to be crafted and rehearsed for maximum effect. They cannot be more than two to three minutes long. This is the structure I use, and it's effective:

- What is the problem?
- What is the solution (make it brief)?
- What are the measurable results (from your current clients)?

"I don't like your manager."

How would you counter this objection?

Do Say

- Thanks for telling me that. That's why I'm here. What was it that caused you not to like the manager?
- Can you explain to me what happened? Is this something I can help resolve?

Don't Say

- I respect your opinion. But the real conversation we should be having is what I can do to help you grow your business.
- Now wait a minute. Do you like every item on a restaurant's menu? I don't think so. You still eat there, right? Well, I am a different person on the menu. Let's talk business!
- Quite frankly, I think the manager is an idiot. We're on the same page with that one.

Stepp's Tip: "I don't like your manager."

This is a perfect example of an objection that sometimes causes salespeople to undermine their company and look completely unprofessional. You should never throw your coworker under the bus. This always backfires and makes you look untrustworthy. And it doesn't solve anything. Coworkers will drop the ball, but tomorrow you may drop the ball. And some coworkers have poor relationship skills and say or do things that don't sit well with buyers. In any case, never, never, never bad-mouth your company or a coworker.

What you want to do is stop selling your idea and start listening to the story behind this objection. The fact that you're interested will cause buyers to open up. If they don't want to open up, don't push the issue. Just follow up in a few weeks and try to get into a conversation about how valuable your product or service is despite their opinion of your manager.

NOTES

Objection #29

"E-mail it to me. I'll call you when I'm ready."

How would you counter this objection?

Do Say

- You're telling me to send you my literature and I'd love to do that. I'd also like a guarantee you're going to look it over so let's set an appointment for next week to discuss any questions you may have.
- I'd be happy to e-mail you. Our packet contains a lot of information, and I don't want to overload you. Do you mind if I ask you just a couple of quick questions so I can send only the specific information that you'd be most interested in?"

Don't Say

- Are you kidding me? You probably won't even read my e-mail. I think you're just blowing me off, so I don't really want to send you anything! Let's just talk about it now.

Stepp's Tip: "E-mail it to me. I'll call you when I'm ready."

How do you handle this type of stall? I suggest you call their bluff. Many salespeople simply take this "e-mail it to me" objection and comply with the request. It's okay to comply with prospects, but do it on your terms. Test the waters with the counters above. If they don't give you an answer, you can do the following:

- Send just enough information to get them interested in knowing more.

- Send a letter with your contact information attached.

If the prospects are genuine in their response, they won't mind answering your questions. So test the waters before you send loads of material that will most likely overload them and get overlooked.

NOTES

Objection #30

"Your company messed things up last time."

How would you counter this objection?

Do Say

- I'm so sorry! That's why I'm here. Can you tell me what happened?
- Can you tell me what went wrong? Once I know the full story, let me see if I can make things right.
- That's why I have an installation checklist. We've changed some of our processes based on feedback from our clients. This checklist, along with key contact numbers, will keep you informed so we don't drop the ball.

Don't Say

- You know your company isn't perfect. We aren't perfect either. So give me a break and let me earn your business.
- How do you handle these situations when they come up in your business? You drop the ball too, so lighten up a little.

Stepp's Tip: "Your company messed things up last time."

When your company drops the ball on buyers, the worst thing you can do is ignore what they have to say about it. I have seen many salespeople completely ignore what a buyer is trying to tell them. The best response is to acknowledge the statement and ask for clarification.

Listening to people doesn't mean you're waiting for your turn to talk. Blowing by an objection like this will confirm that you aren't the company to do business with. Slow down and find out what happened. You don't have to agree with what they said. You only need to listen and put yourself in their shoes by using effective empathy statements.

If you were the buyer and this happened to you, wouldn't you react the same way? Listening and repeating back to prospects what they say lowers their frustration and brings your relationship to a neutral position. You can always go up from there. Trying to give buyers instructions when they have issues with your company opens up the possibility of hostility toward you.

NOTES

Objection #31

"I told my friends I'd use their company."

How would you counter this objection?

Do Say

- Thanks for letting me know. Can you explain what problem this solution will solve? Do you think their company will be able to handle all phases of this process?
- That's great. We can let them handle the major project. Would you like to see if there is something specific I can help you with that may work with your friend's services or benefit you as well as their plan?

Don't Say

- You know what happens with a *friend* deal, don't you? Playing family politics can get you fired. Do you really want to risk your job?

Stepp's Tip: "I told my friends I'd use their company."

This objection is a common one. The goal isn't to boot the competition out. That would end up working against you. Don't challenge prospects' decisions either. Instead, praise them for their choice. Thank them for letting you know. Then ask questions that will uncover other business problems you may be able to solve. You may not be able to do anything for them at this time, but stay in touch and see how the project is coming along. Down the road, if there is a failure in service or product, the buyer will be glad you stayed in touch. The friendly relationship could eventually turn sour, and you want to be first in line to pick up the ball if that happens.

Objection #32

"Is this the best price I can get?"

How would you counter this objection?

Do Say

- Yes, this is the best price you can get! (Pause and wait for a response.)
- I can give you a better price, but we'll need to see what options you want to exclude from the package.
- I already discounted the price for this product (or service) up front because you mentioned, in our last conversation, about the budget that you can't exceed. Here is the amount of discount I applied.

Don't Say

- Sure, take another 20 percent off. I knew you were going to say something like this.
- You're driving a $100,000 car. I think you can afford this price.

Stepp's Tip: "Is this the best price I can get?

This is one of the most common price objections. The best response is to tell them *yes*, this is the best price. Then wait for their response. In many cases, prospects are going to buy from you either way. Pause after the question and see what happens. If their second response is another objection, you know there's an opportunity to negotiate the deal until both parties have a win-win outcome.

Muscle-Up Activity

"Is this the best price I can get?"

Remember the story at the start of this book about my brave, daring exchange at the coffee shop?

Well, I encourage *you* to take the challenge.

Over the next few weeks, ask this any time you purchase something in person or on the phone. Before a cashier scans the item, ask him or her, "Is this the best price I can get?"

Do this at the grocery store, coffee shop, diner, restaurant, movie, tire shop, furniture store … I mean anywhere and everywhere!

Look for the following:

- How do they respond? Most don't know what to say and will either get the manager or give a discount immediately.
- Watch how they say it. Did they say it with confidence, pride, and strength, or were they annoyed or confused? Watch body language when they respond.
- If you can't do this, why not? What are you telling yourself? Are you self-conscious or a people pleaser? Does this embarrass you? Ask yourself why you can't negotiate for your own money. Remember—cultures all over the world negotiate and barter for their daily tasks and purchases.

Learning how to object quickly and answer quickly is a natural process for many people. You can do the same, but you must practice in the marketplace and in your personal life. You'll be amazed at the results.

Available Now

Survive or Thrive?

Book and Workbook

Survive or Thrive? Creating the Life You Want Out of the Life You Have

Stepp Stevens Sydnor with Suzi Streit

Survive or Thrive? Creating the Life You Want Out of the Life You Have is an eye-opening, motivational book that helps readers move from survival mode into a thriving and more fulfilling existence. Author Stepp Stevens Sydnor offers personal accounts as well as helpful instruction on how to rethink situations in order to create a better life. From the seven characteristics of a thriver to sound advice on how to truly bounce back after trials, *Survive or Thrive?* teaches readers lessons that can be applied throughout their businesses, relationships, and entire lives.

Available at www.amazon.com.

2 **Meeting Close**
Selling System

More Confidence   **More Sales**   **More Freedom**

The 2 Meeting Close Selling System will teach you

- how to close a deal in two meetings or less
- how to capture prospects' attention in 3 seconds
- how to control the meeting outcome
- how to turn a maybe into a YES
- how to cut your sales cycle down 25%
- how to create business deals faster
- how to minimize the price pressure
- how to look more professional
- how to create solutions and demand
- how to break prospects' preoccupation
- how to turn commodity products into high dollar solutions

Schedule a workshop today to learn

how to create and close business in two meetings or less

Call **(903) 539-6840**

www.2MeetingClose.com

By Stepp Sydnor
Author / Speaker / Performance Coach
Stepp has delivered thousands of motivational presentations, seminars, and meetings. He has developed nine seminars for leadership and sales effectiveness and has authored two books which have won three acclaimed publishing awards. Stepp mixes enthusiasm and humor with true life stories in this system he perfected to close business in two meetings or less. His high-power messages and practical content empowers his audience with a confidence to get extraordinary results in their sales performance. Stepp began his sales career after college in Dallas, TX and has over thirty years of experience in business-to-business sales and marketing.

Book Stepp Stevens Sydnor for your next event

Contact information for Stepp Stevens Sydnor

Mailing:

Stepp Stevens Sydnor
PO Box 2201
Rockwall TX 75087

E-mail: stepp@2meetingclose.com

Call: 903-539-6840

Website: www.2meetingclose.com

Look for Stepp's next book, fall of 2016:

2 Meeting Close: How to Close Business in 2 Meetings or Less

Printed in the United States
By Bookmasters